THE SUPERPOWER OF YOUR HEART

WRITTEN BY LINDSEY FRANK   ART BY SAM HINTZ

Custom Art illustrations by Sam Hintz
Edited by Jolinda Cappello

Printed in the United States of America
Lindsey J. Frank, The Butterfly Within, 2022
ISBN 978-1-7351833-4-3
Library of Congress Control Number: 2022901227

For additional companion resources and to contact for permission,
please visit:

www.TheButterflyWithin.Me

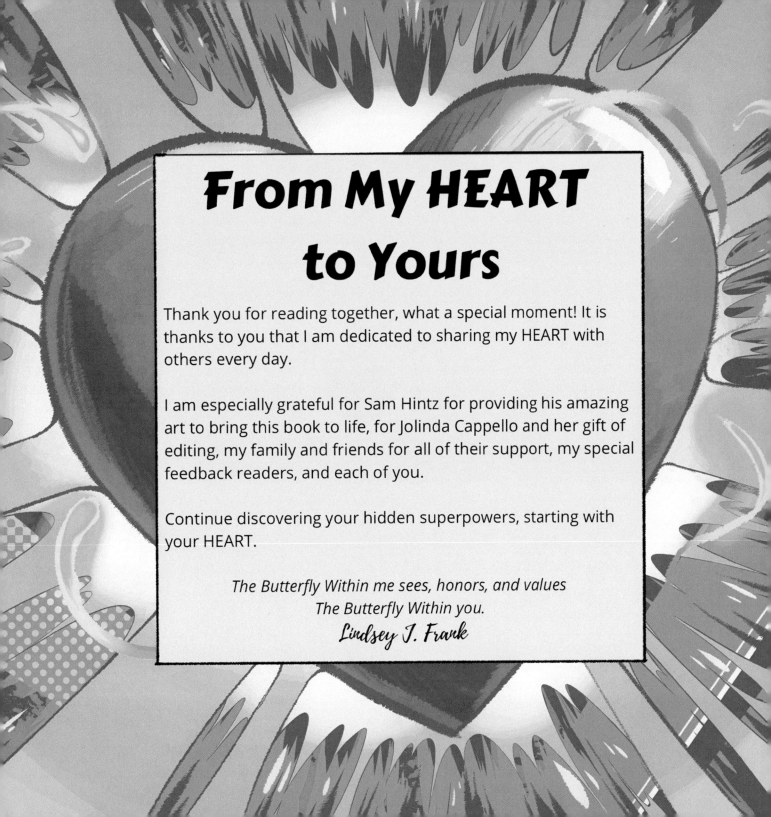

From My HEART to Yours

Thank you for reading together, what a special moment! It is thanks to you that I am dedicated to sharing my HEART with others every day.

I am especially grateful for Sam Hintz for providing his amazing art to bring this book to life, for Jolinda Cappello and her gift of editing, my family and friends for all of their support, my special feedback readers, and each of you.

Continue discovering your hidden superpowers, starting with your HEART.

The Butterfly Within me sees, honors, and values
The Butterfly Within you.

Lindsey J. Frank

IMPORTANT!!!!!

When you see this symbol,
visit
www.TheButterflyWithin.Me/superpower

The Superpower of Your HEART is inspired by an emotional regulation and wellness tool called HEART. The acronym, **HEART**, stands for:

Health, **E**nvironment, **A**ffirmation, **R**esponse, **T**ransform

It combines mindfulness with social and emotional learning (SEL) so that you can remain aware and regulated within any situation, anytime, anywhere.

This highly interactive book is written in the form of an SEL lesson and is meant to be the first step for introducing your HEART's superpower. Find connected teaching tools, scenarios, resources, and coaching for continued learning on the website.

Family and Educator Connection

Helpful Talking Points

- Our body is always communicating with us. It takes practice to be able to listen to your body's (and HEART's) messages.
- One way we can connect with our HEART is through mindfulness.
  - *Mindfulness means being fully present with your body, breath, emotions, and thoughts with a sense of curiosity and openness.*
- Sometimes we may feel worried, anxious, upset, frustrated, or uncertain. These are great times to **"Check in with your HEART."** You can check in with your HEART all the time, even when you are feeling awesome!
  - *When during the day would it be helpful to check in with your HEART?*
- An **acronym** takes the first letter of different words, puts the letters together, creates a new word, and helps us remember a tricky idea. HEART is the acronym for this book.
- Sometimes there are BIG words you may not know. If you see a BIG word, you can ask, *"What does _____ mean?"*

Teaching Tips

- **Add HEART Into <u>Your</u> Life:** Model this skill for your children/students.
  - *Notice the impact it has on your life as well!*
- **Pre-Teaching:** Consider teaching your children/students the BIG words before reading together.
  - *Resources available at:* **www.TheButterflyWithin.Me/superpower**
- **One Word A Day:** After reading, keep adding the next word until HEART can be fully integrated.
- **Create a Schedule:** Schedule times during your (school) day to *"Check in with your HEART"* and guide everyone through the steps.
- **Prompting:** When children/students appear to be outside of their Button Zone, prompt them to check in with their HEART to help them get back into a calmer and more regulated state.

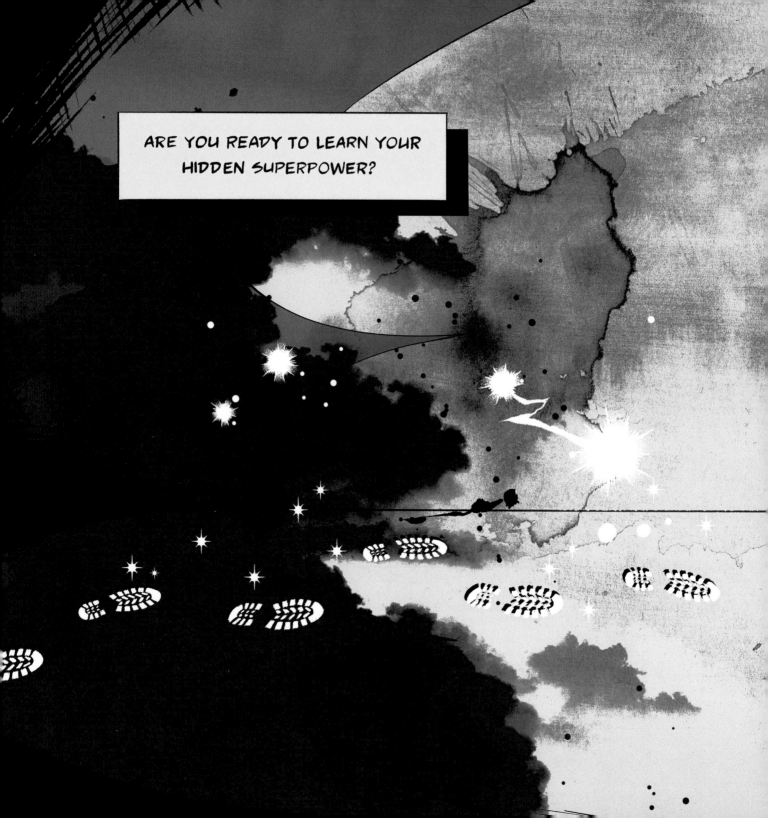

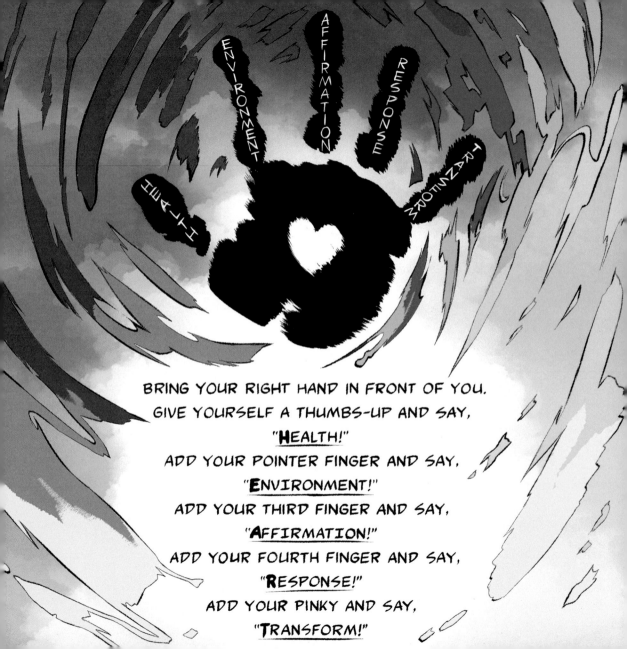

BRING YOUR RIGHT HAND IN FRONT OF YOU.
GIVE YOURSELF A THUMBS-UP AND SAY,
"HEALTH!"
ADD YOUR POINTER FINGER AND SAY,
"ENVIRONMENT!"
ADD YOUR THIRD FINGER AND SAY,
"AFFIRMATION!"
ADD YOUR FOURTH FINGER AND SAY,
"RESPONSE!"
ADD YOUR PINKY AND SAY,
"TRANSFORM!"

TRACE YOUR HAND BELOW AND WRITE THE CODE WORDS ON EACH FINGER.

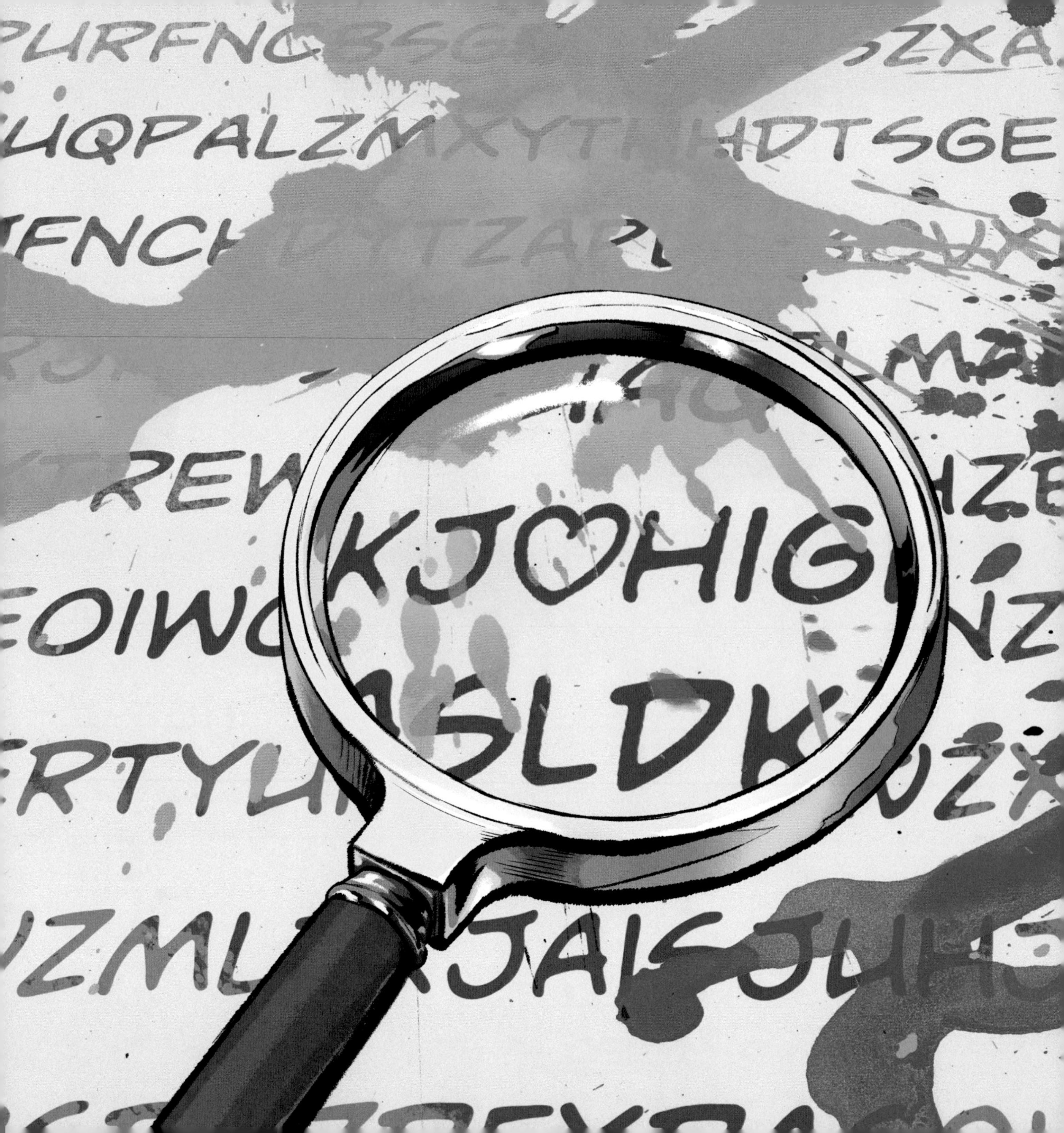
KJOHIG
SLDK

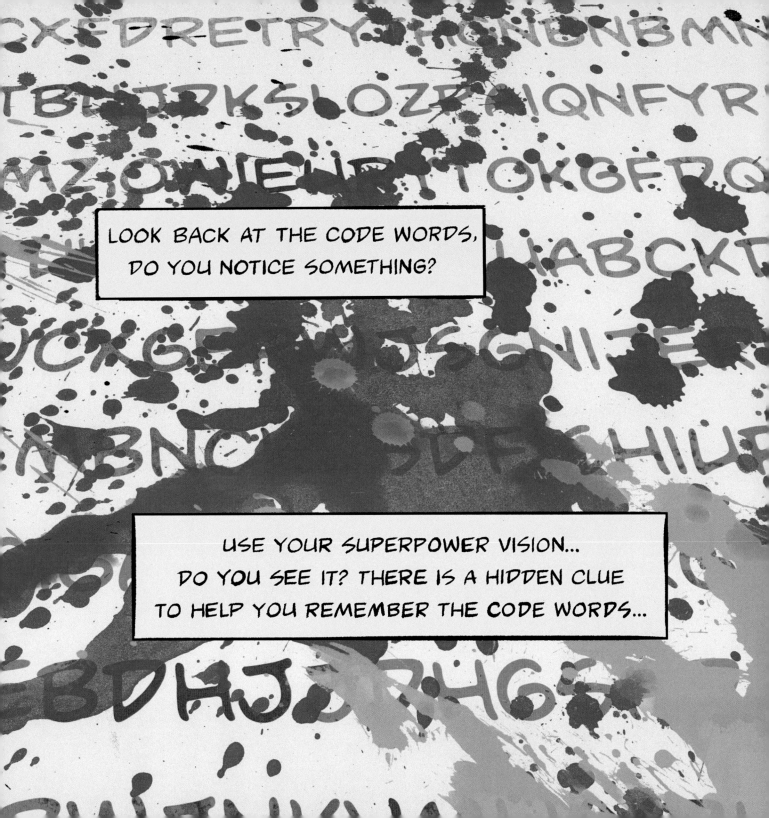

THE QUESTIONS HELP YOU
TO KNOW THE HIDDEN MESSAGES YOUR
HEART SHARES WITH YOU.

KNOWING THE MESSAGES HELPS YOU
TO STAY IN CONTROL OF ANY SITUATION
TO MAKE A SUPERHERO CHOICE.

LET'S TRY IT!

CHECK IN WITH YOUR **HEART**:

1 - PLACE YOUR HAND ON YOUR **HEART**.
2 - BREATHE IN AND BREATHE OUT.
3 - SAY EACH CODE WORD AND ASK ITS SPECIAL QUESTION.
4 - PAUSE AFTER EACH QUESTION AND SEE WHAT MESSAGES YOUR **HEART** SHARES.
5 - CHOOSE YOUR ACTION.
6 - BREATHE IN AND BREATHE OUT.

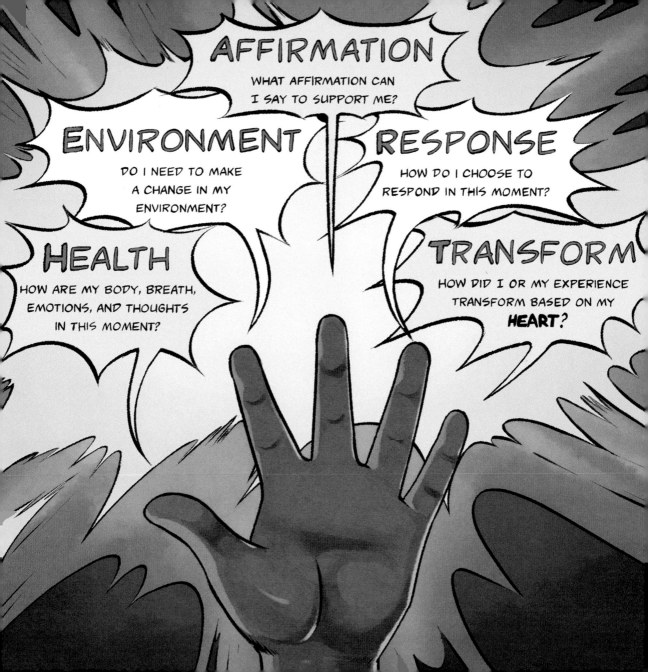

WAIT!

DO <u>NOT</u> TURN THIS PAGE, YET!

FOLLOW ANY MESSAGES THAT YOUR **HEART** SHARED WITH YOU.

TAKE CHARGE OF YOUR SUPERPOWER!

...TAKE **ACTION!**

LET'S CELEBRATE
THE SUPERPOWER OF YOUR HEART!

LEADER: MY HEART IS STRONG!

EVERYONE: MY HEART IS STRONG!

LEADER: MY HEART IS POWERFUL!

EVERYONE: MY HEART IS POWERFUL!

LEADER: I AM STRONG!

EVERYONE: I AM STRONG!

LEADER: I AM POWERFUL!

EVERYONE: I AM POWERFUL!

LEADER: MY HEART GUIDES ME!

EVERYONE: MY HEART GUIDES ME!

LEADER: I LISTEN AND FOLLOW!

EVERYONE: I LISTEN AND FOLLOW!

**EVERYONE: NO MATTER THE DAY,
NO MATTER THE TIME, MY POWER IS READY,
AND I WILL BE JUST FINE!**

BE THE SUPERHERO WITHIN YOUR HEART!

DRAW YOURSELF AS A SUPERHERO, ADD THE SPECIAL CODE WORDS, AND WRITE WHEN YOU CAN USE YOUR SUPERPOWER TODAY!

SUPERHERO CHALLENGE: IN YOUR DRAWING, ADD YOUR SIDEKICKS (THE IMPORTANT PEOPLE WHO CAN HELP YOU TO FOLLOW YOUR HEART).

NEXT STEP

See how to use your superpower in action!

Visit:
www.TheButterflyWithin.Me/superpower

Share & Follow
Share your superpower creations and stories on social media to inspire others!

Twitter: @LindseyFrank88 @SamDrawsCartoon
Instagram: @LindseyFrank88 @SamDrawsCartoons
Facebook: @TheButterflyWithin @SamDrawsDaCartoons

#TheButterflyWithin

Lindsey Frank, M.Ed., is dedicated to connecting with children, their families, and education professionals around the world. She has taught and supported students ranging from early learning through junior high across diverse learning environments. Her passion is connecting teaching practices, wellness, and social and emotional learning within education. She is a well-being coach, mindfulness and meditation teacher, and certified yoga instructor for adults and children.

Lindsey is the author of *Big Change, Better You, Beautiful World* and is published in *Educating Mindfully: Stories of School Transformation Through Mindfulness.*

SAM Hintz is an illustrator with a fine arts degree from the School of the Art Institute of Chicago. He's been making drawings for children's books for 5 years that visually show the importance of diversity, inclusivity, creativity, robots, fireballs, and other cool stuff.

SAM is the author and illustrator of *The Most Monstrous Band.*

The Butterfly Within me sees, honors, and values The Butterfly Within you.

Made in the USA
Monee, IL
22 September 2022

14316308R00029